Beatrix Po

The Peter Rabbit
Password Logbook

- Passwordbook -

This book is property of	
Name, Firstname:	
Street / nr.:	
Postal Code (Zip) / Town:	
Phone:	
Email:	
Notes:	

Bibliografische Information der Deutschen Nationalbibliothek:
Die Deutsche Nationalbibliothek verzeichnet diese Publikation in der Deutschen Nationalbibliografie;
detaillierte bibliografische Daten sind im Internet über http://dnb.dnb.de abrufbar.

Texts und Illustrations/ Covergraphic: © Elizabeth M. Potter

Herstellung und Verlag: BoD – Books on Demand, Norderstedt

ISBN: 9783752866575

Titel:
Web Address:
Login / User:
Password / Pin:
Notes / recovery question / pass phrase / Hint:

Titel:
Web Address:
Login / User:
Password / Pin:
Notes / recovery question / pass phrase / Hint:

Titel:
Web Address:
Login / User:
Password / Pin:
Notes / recovery question / pass phrase / Hint:

Titel:

Web Address:

Login / User:

Password / Pin:

Notes / recovery question / pass phrase / Hint:

Titel:

Web Address:

Login / User:

Password / Pin:

Notes / recovery question / pass phrase / Hint:

Titel:

Web Address:

Login / User:

Password / Pin:

Notes / recovery question / pass phrase / Hint:

Titel:

Web Address:

Login / User:

Password / Pin:

Notes / recovery question / pass phrase / Hint:

Titel:

Web Address:

Login / User:

Password / Pin:

Notes / recovery question / pass phrase / Hint:

Titel:

Web Address:

Login / User:

Password / Pin:

Notes / recovery question / pass phrase / Hint:

Titel:
Web Address:
Login / User:
Password / Pin:
Notes / recovery question / pass phrase / Hint:

Titel:
Web Address:
Login / User:
Password / Pin:
Notes / recovery question / pass phrase / Hint:

Titel:
Web Address:
Login / User:
Password / Pin:
Notes / recovery question / pass phrase / Hint:

Titel:

Web Address:

Login / User:

Password / Pin:

Notes / recovery question / pass phrase / Hint:

Titel:

Web Address:

Login / User:

Password / Pin:

Notes / recovery question / pass phrase / Hint:

Titel:

Web Address:

Login / User:

Password / Pin:

Notes / recovery question / pass phrase / Hint:

Titel:
Web Address:
Login / User:
Password / Pin:
Notes / recovery question / pass phrase / Hint:

Titel:
Web Address:
Login / User:
Password / Pin:
Notes / recovery question / pass phrase / Hint:

Titel:
Web Address:
Login / User:
Password / Pin:
Notes / recovery question / pass phrase / Hint:

Titel:

Web Address:

Login / User:

Password / Pin:

Notes / recovery question / pass phrase / Hint:

Titel:

Web Address:

Login / User:

Password / Pin:

Notes / recovery question / pass phrase / Hint:

Titel:

Web Address:

Login / User:

Password / Pin:

Notes / recovery question / pass phrase / Hint:

Titel:
Web Address:
Login / User:
Password / Pin:
Notes / recovery question / pass phrase / Hint:

Titel:
Web Address:
Login / User:
Password / Pin:
Notes / recovery question / pass phrase / Hint:

Titel:
Web Address:
Login / User:
Password / Pin:
Notes / recovery question / pass phrase / Hint:

Titel:
Web Address:
Login / User:
Password / Pin:
Notes / recovery question / pass phrase / Hint:

Titel:
Web Address:
Login / User:
Password / Pin:
Notes / recovery question / pass phrase / Hint:

Titel:
Web Address:
Login / User:
Password / Pin:
Notes / recovery question / pass phrase / Hint:

Titel:

Web Address:

Login / User:

Password / Pin:

Notes / recovery question / pass phrase / Hint:

Titel:

Web Address:

Login / User:

Password / Pin:

Notes / recovery question / pass phrase / Hint:

Titel:

Web Address:

Login / User:

Password / Pin:

Notes / recovery question / pass phrase / Hint:

Titel:
Web Address:
Login / User:
Password / Pin:
Notes / recovery question / pass phrase / Hint:

Titel:
Web Address:
Login / User:
Password / Pin:
Notes / recovery question / pass phrase / Hint:

Titel:
Web Address:
Login / User:
Password / Pin:
Notes / recovery question / pass phrase / Hint:

Titel:

Web Address:

Login / User:

Password / Pin:

Notes / recovery question / pass phrase / Hint:

Titel:

Web Address:

Login / User:

Password / Pin:

Notes / recovery question / pass phrase / Hint:

Titel:

Web Address:

Login / User:

Password / Pin:

Notes / recovery question / pass phrase / Hint:

Titel:

Web Address:

Login / User:

Password / Pin:

Notes / recovery question / pass phrase / Hint:

Titel:

Web Address:

Login / User:

Password / Pin:

Notes / recovery question / pass phrase / Hint:

Titel:

Web Address:

Login / User:

Password / Pin:

Notes / recovery question / pass phrase / Hint:

Titel:
Web Address:
Login / User:
Password / Pin:
Notes / recovery question / pass phrase / Hint:

Titel:
Web Address:
Login / User:
Password / Pin:
Notes / recovery question / pass phrase / Hint:

Titel:
Web Address:
Login / User:
Password / Pin:
Notes / recovery question / pass phrase / Hint:

Titel:
Web Address:
Login / User:
Password / Pin:
Notes / recovery question / pass phrase / Hint:

Titel:
Web Address:
Login / User:
Password / Pin:
Notes / recovery question / pass phrase / Hint:

Titel:
Web Address:
Login / User:
Password / Pin:
Notes / recovery question / pass phrase / Hint:

Titel:

Web Address:

Login / User:

Password / Pin:

Notes / recovery question / pass phrase / Hint:

Titel:

Web Address:

Login / User:

Password / Pin:

Notes / recovery question / pass phrase / Hint:

Titel:

Web Address:

Login / User:

Password / Pin:

Notes / recovery question / pass phrase / Hint:

Titel:

Web Address:

Login / User:

Password / Pin:

Notes / recovery question / pass phrase / Hint:

Titel:

Web Address:

Login / User:

Password / Pin:

Notes / recovery question / pass phrase / Hint:

Titel:

Web Address:

Login / User:

Password / Pin:

Notes / recovery question / pass phrase / Hint:

Titel:

Web Address:

Login / User:

Password / Pin:

Notes / recovery question / pass phrase / Hint:

Titel:

Web Address:

Login / User:

Password / Pin:

Notes / recovery question / pass phrase / Hint:

Titel:

Web Address:

Login / User:

Password / Pin:

Notes / recovery question / pass phrase / Hint:

Titel:
Web Address:
Login / User:
Password / Pin:
Notes / recovery question / pass phrase / Hint:

Titel:
Web Address:
Login / User:
Password / Pin:
Notes / recovery question / pass phrase / Hint:

Titel:
Web Address:
Login / User:
Password / Pin:
Notes / recovery question / pass phrase / Hint:

Titel:

Web Address:

Login / User:

Password / Pin:

Notes / recovery question / pass phrase / Hint:

Titel:

Web Address:

Login / User:

Password / Pin:

Notes / recovery question / pass phrase / Hint:

Titel:

Web Address:

Login / User:

Password / Pin:

Notes / recovery question / pass phrase / Hint:

Titel:

Web Address:

Login / User:

Password / Pin:

Notes / recovery question / pass phrase / Hint:

Titel:

Web Address:

Login / User:

Password / Pin:

Notes / recovery question / pass phrase / Hint:

Titel:

Web Address:

Login / User:

Password / Pin:

Notes / recovery question / pass phrase / Hint:

Titel:
Web Address:
Login / User:
Password / Pin:
Notes / recovery question / pass phrase / Hint:

Titel:
Web Address:
Login / User:
Password / Pin:
Notes / recovery question / pass phrase / Hint:

Titel:
Web Address:
Login / User:
Password / Pin:
Notes / recovery question / pass phrase / Hint:

Titel:
Web Address:
Login / User:
Password / Pin:
Notes / recovery question / pass phrase / Hint:

Titel:
Web Address:
Login / User:
Password / Pin:
Notes / recovery question / pass phrase / Hint:

Titel:
Web Address:
Login / User:
Password / Pin:
Notes / recovery question / pass phrase / Hint:

Titel:
Web Address:
Login / User:
Password / Pin:
Notes / recovery question / pass phrase / Hint:

Titel:
Web Address:
Login / User:
Password / Pin:
Notes / recovery question / pass phrase / Hint:

Titel:
Web Address:
Login / User:
Password / Pin:
Notes / recovery question / pass phrase / Hint:

Titel:
Web Address:
Login / User:
Password / Pin:
Notes / recovery question / pass phrase / Hint:

Titel:
Web Address:
Login / User:
Password / Pin:
Notes / recovery question / pass phrase / Hint:

Titel:
Web Address:
Login / User:
Password / Pin:
Notes / recovery question / pass phrase / Hint:

Titel:
Web Address:
Login / User:
Password / Pin:
Notes / recovery question / pass phrase / Hint:

Titel:
Web Address:
Login / User:
Password / Pin:
Notes / recovery question / pass phrase / Hint:

Titel:
Web Address:
Login / User:
Password / Pin:
Notes / recovery question / pass phrase / Hint:

Titel:
Web Address:
Login / User:
Password / Pin:
Notes / recovery question / pass phrase / Hint:

Titel:
Web Address:
Login / User:
Password / Pin:
Notes / recovery question / pass phrase / Hint:

Titel:
Web Address:
Login / User:
Password / Pin:
Notes / recovery question / pass phrase / Hint:

Titel:
Web Address:
Login / User:
Password / Pin:
Notes / recovery question / pass phrase / Hint:

Titel:
Web Address:
Login / User:
Password / Pin:
Notes / recovery question / pass phrase / Hint:

Titel:
Web Address:
Login / User:
Password / Pin:
Notes / recovery question / pass phrase / Hint:

Titel:

Web Address:

Login / User:

Password / Pin:

Notes / recovery question / pass phrase / Hint:

Titel:

Web Address:

Login / User:

Password / Pin:

Notes / recovery question / pass phrase / Hint:

Titel:

Web Address:

Login / User:

Password / Pin:

Notes / recovery question / pass phrase / Hint:

Titel:

Web Address:

Login / User:

Password / Pin:

Notes / recovery question / pass phrase / Hint:

Titel:

Web Address:

Login / User:

Password / Pin:

Notes / recovery question / pass phrase / Hint:

Titel:

Web Address:

Login / User:

Password / Pin:

Notes / recovery question / pass phrase / Hint:

Titel:
Web Address:
Login / User:
Password / Pin:
Notes / recovery question / pass phrase / Hint:

Titel:
Web Address:
Login / User:
Password / Pin:
Notes / recovery question / pass phrase / Hint:

Titel:
Web Address:
Login / User:
Password / Pin:
Notes / recovery question / pass phrase / Hint:

Titel:

Web Address:

Login / User:

Password / Pin:

Notes / recovery question / pass phrase / Hint:

Titel:

Web Address:

Login / User:

Password / Pin:

Notes / recovery question / pass phrase / Hint:

Titel:

Web Address:

Login / User:

Password / Pin:

Notes / recovery question / pass phrase / Hint:

Titel:
Web Address:
Login / User:
Password / Pin:
Notes / recovery question / pass phrase / Hint:

Titel:
Web Address:
Login / User:
Password / Pin:
Notes / recovery question / pass phrase / Hint:

Titel:
Web Address:
Login / User:
Password / Pin:
Notes / recovery question / pass phrase / Hint:

Titel:
Web Address:
Login / User:
Password / Pin:
Notes / recovery question / pass phrase / Hint:

Titel:
Web Address:
Login / User:
Password / Pin:
Notes / recovery question / pass phrase / Hint:

Titel:
Web Address:
Login / User:
Password / Pin:
Notes / recovery question / pass phrase / Hint:

Titel:
Web Address:
Login / User:
Password / Pin:
Notes / recovery question / pass phrase / Hint:

Titel:
Web Address:
Login / User:
Password / Pin:
Notes / recovery question / pass phrase / Hint:

Titel:
Web Address:
Login / User:
Password / Pin:
Notes / recovery question / pass phrase / Hint:

Titel:

Web Address:

Login / User:

Password / Pin:

Notes / recovery question / pass phrase / Hint:

Titel:

Web Address:

Login / User:

Password / Pin:

Notes / recovery question / pass phrase / Hint:

Titel:

Web Address:

Login / User:

Password / Pin:

Notes / recovery question / pass phrase / Hint:

Titel:

Web Address:

Login / User:

Password / Pin:

Notes / recovery question / pass phrase / Hint:

Titel:

Web Address:

Login / User:

Password / Pin:

Notes / recovery question / pass phrase / Hint:

Titel:

Web Address:

Login / User:

Password / Pin:

Notes / recovery question / pass phrase / Hint:

Titel:
Web Address:
Login / User:
Password / Pin:
Notes / recovery question / pass phrase / Hint:

Titel:
Web Address:
Login / User:
Password / Pin:
Notes / recovery question / pass phrase / Hint:

Titel:
Web Address:
Login / User:
Password / Pin:
Notes / recovery question / pass phrase / Hint:

Titel:
Web Address:
Login / User:
Password / Pin:
Notes / recovery question / pass phrase / Hint:

Titel:
Web Address:
Login / User:
Password / Pin:
Notes / recovery question / pass phrase / Hint:

Titel:
Web Address:
Login / User:
Password / Pin:
Notes / recovery question / pass phrase / Hint:

Titel:

Web Address:

Login / User:

Password / Pin:

Notes / recovery question / pass phrase / Hint:

Titel:

Web Address:

Login / User:

Password / Pin:

Notes / recovery question / pass phrase / Hint:

Titel:

Web Address:

Login / User:

Password / Pin:

Notes / recovery question / pass phrase / Hint:

Titel:

Web Address:

Login / User:

Password / Pin:

Notes / recovery question / pass phrase / Hint:

Titel:

Web Address:

Login / User:

Password / Pin:

Notes / recovery question / pass phrase / Hint:

Titel:

Web Address:

Login / User:

Password / Pin:

Notes / recovery question / pass phrase / Hint:

Titel:
Web Address:
Login / User:
Password / Pin:
Notes / recovery question / pass phrase / Hint:

Titel:
Web Address:
Login / User:
Password / Pin:
Notes / recovery question / pass phrase / Hint:

Titel:
Web Address:
Login / User:
Password / Pin:
Notes / recovery question / pass phrase / Hint:

Titel:

Web Address:

Login / User:

Password / Pin:

Notes / recovery question / pass phrase / Hint:

Titel:

Web Address:

Login / User:

Password / Pin:

Notes / recovery question / pass phrase / Hint:

Titel:

Web Address:

Login / User:

Password / Pin:

Notes / recovery question / pass phrase / Hint:

Titel:

Web Address:

Login / User:

Password / Pin:

Notes / recovery question / pass phrase / Hint:

Titel:

Web Address:

Login / User:

Password / Pin:

Notes / recovery question / pass phrase / Hint:

Titel:

Web Address:

Login / User:

Password / Pin:

Notes / recovery question / pass phrase / Hint:

Titel:	
Web Address:	
Login / User:	
Password / Pin:	
Notes / recovery question / pass phrase / Hint:	

Titel:	
Web Address:	
Login / User:	
Password / Pin:	
Notes / recovery question / pass phrase / Hint:	

Titel:	
Web Address:	
Login / User:	
Password / Pin:	
Notes / recovery question / pass phrase / Hint:	

Titel:

Web Address:

Login / User:

Password / Pin:

Notes / recovery question / pass phrase / Hint:

Titel:

Web Address:

Login / User:

Password / Pin:

Notes / recovery question / pass phrase / Hint:

Titel:

Web Address:

Login / User:

Password / Pin:

Notes / recovery question / pass phrase / Hint:

Titel:

Web Address:

Login / User:

Password / Pin:

Notes / recovery question / pass phrase / Hint:

Titel:

Web Address:

Login / User:

Password / Pin:

Notes / recovery question / pass phrase / Hint:

Titel:

Web Address:

Login / User:

Password / Pin:

Notes / recovery question / pass phrase / Hint:

Titel:

Web Address:

Login / User:

Password / Pin:

Notes / recovery question / pass phrase / Hint:

Titel:

Web Address:

Login / User:

Password / Pin:

Notes / recovery question / pass phrase / Hint:

Titel:

Web Address:

Login / User:

Password / Pin:

Notes / recovery question / pass phrase / Hint:

Titel:

Web Address:

Login / User:

Password / Pin:

Notes / recovery question / pass phrase / Hint:

Titel:

Web Address:

Login / User:

Password / Pin:

Notes / recovery question / pass phrase / Hint:

Titel:

Web Address:

Login / User:

Password / Pin:

Notes / recovery question / pass phrase / Hint:

Titel:
Web Address:
Login / User:
Password / Pin:
Notes / recovery question / pass phrase / Hint:

Titel:
Web Address:
Login / User:
Password / Pin:
Notes / recovery question / pass phrase / Hint:

Titel:
Web Address:
Login / User:
Password / Pin:
Notes / recovery question / pass phrase / Hint:

Titel: Email (Private):
eMail Server Type:
Server (incoming):
Server (outgoing):
Login / User:
Password / Pin:

Titel: Email:
eMail Server Type:
Server (incoming):
Server (outgoing):
Login / User:
Password / Pin:

Titel: Internet Service Provider (ISP) Support
Name ISP:
Web address ISP:
Customer Number:
Hotline Customer Support:
Email Customer Support:
Web Address Customer Support:

Titel: Email (Private):
eMail Server Type:
Server (incoming):
Server (outgoing):
Login / User:
Password / Pin:

Titel: Email:
eMail Server Type:
Server (incoming):
Server (outgoing):
Login / User:
Password / Pin:

Titel: Internet Service Provider (ISP) Support
Name ISP:
Web address ISP:
Customer Number:
Hotline Customer Support:
Email Customer Support:
Web Address Customer Support:

Titel: broadband Modem	Titel: Configuration WLAN
Model:	Host name:
Factory nr.:	Domain name:
Mac Address:	Subnet Mask:
URL/IP Admin:	gateway:
IP WAN:	DNS (Primary):
Login/User:	DNS (Secondary):
Password:	

Titel: Router / Wireless Access Point
Model:
Factory number:
Factory Setting Admin IP:
Factory Setting Username:
Factory Setting Password:
User defined Admin URL /IP:
User defined Username:
User defined Password:

Titel: Wireless-LAN
SSID / Name WLAN Network:
Security Type:
Encryption Type:
Shared key (WPA):
Hint (Passphrase WEP):

Titel: broadband Modem	Titel: Configuration WLAN
Model:	Host name:
Factory nr.:	Domain name:
Mac Address:	Subnet Mask:
URL/IP Admin:	gateway:
IP WAN:	DNS (Primary):
Login/User:	DNS (Secondary):
Password:	

Titel: Router / Wireless Access Point
Model:
Factory number:
Factory Setting Admin IP:
Factory Setting Username:
Factory Setting Password:
User defined Admin URL /IP:
User defined Username:
User defined Password:

Titel: Wireless-LAN
SSID / Name WLAN Network:
Security Type:
Encryption Type:
Shared key (WPA):
Hint (Passphrase WEP):

Notes:

Notes:

Notes:

Further books of Elizabeth M. Potter

NOTEBOOKS
The Peter Rabbit Notebook
PAINTING BOOKS
Beatrix Potter Painting Book Part 1 (Peter Rabbit)
Beatrix Potter Painting Book Part 2 (Peter Rabbit)
Beatrix Potter Painting Book Part 3 (Peter Rabbit)
Beatrix Potter Painting Book Part 4 (Peter Rabbit)
Beatrix Potter Painting Book Part 5 (Peter Rabbit)
Beatrix Potter Painting Book Part 6 (Peter Rabbit)
Beatrix Potter Painting Book Part 7 (Peter Rabbit)
Beatrix Potter Painting Book Part 8 (Peter Rabbit)
Beatrix Potter Painting Book Part 9 (Peter Rabbit)
Beatrix Potter Painting Book Part 10 (Peter Rabbit)
Peter Rabbit Painting Book
CLIPART BOOKS
Beatrix Potter 99 Cliparts Book Part 1 (Peter Rabbit)
Beatrix Potter 99 Cliparts Book Part 2 (Peter Rabbit)
Beatrix Potter 99 Cliparts Book Part 3 (Peter Rabbit)
Beatrix Potter 99 Cliparts Book Part 4 (Peter Rabbit)
PASSWORD BOOKS
The Peter Rabbit Passwortbook